Nice To See You, Andy Capp!

by
Smythe

A FAWCETT GOLD MEDAL BOOK

Fawcett Publications, Inc., Greenwich, Connecticut

NICE TO SEE YOU, ANDY CAPP!

ANDY CAPP of the Daily Mirror, London

© 1974, 1975 IPC Newspaper Ltd.

© 1977 CBS Publications, The Consumer Publishing
Division of CBS, Inc. All rights reserved

Copyright under International and Pan-American Copyright
Conventions.

Published by special arrangement with Field Newspaper Syndicate.

All inquiries should be addressed to Hall House, Inc.,
262 Mason Street, Greenwich, Connecticut.

ISBN 0-449-13848-8

Printed in the United States of America

10   9   8   7   6   5   4   3   2   1

8-27

'DAD' SHE CALLED ME....!

FLO, YOU 'AVEN'T BEEN SAYIN' ANYTHIN' TO THAT BARMAID ABOUT 'OW OLD I AM, 'AVE YER?

NOT REALLY, PET. JUST IN THE COURSE OF CONVERSATION I MENTIONED THAT WE ARE THE SAME AGE —

OF ALL THE ROTTEN THINGS TO SAY!!

9-10

≳SIGH≲

4-19

THE MOST FASCINATIN' THING ABOUT BOOZE IS WHERE THE BREWERIES FIND ALL THOSE 'APPY PUBS TO FILM THE COMMERCIALS IN—

Smythe

THERE ARE TIMES WHEN 'E FEELS THAT LIFE IS EMPTY AN' MEANINGLESS —

— AN' THEN THE WAITER ARRIVES WITH 'IS ORDER

9-24

YOU'RE ONLY YOUNG ONCE, EH, MISTER CAPP?

TRUE—

AN' AFTER THAT YOU CAN ALWAYS BLAME IT ON THE BOOZE

12:30

.... BE SATISFIED, LAD, THERE'S A LOT TO BE SAID ABOUT MARRIAGE —

.37

THERE *MUST* BE — FLO AN' 'ER MOTHER 'AVEN'T STOPPED TALKIN' ABOUT *OURS* SINCE I *MET* 'EM!

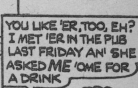

1-6

NO, THANKS, FLO — I KNOW MY LIMIT

1-20

GO AN' TALK TO THE VICAR, PET — 'E ALWAYS SEEMS SO LONELY AN' OUT OF PLACE AT A PARTY

TCH! WHY ME?

NONE OF YER GUESTS SEEM TO FANCY CHATTIN' TO A MAN WI' LETTERS AFTER 'IS NAME

IS IT ANY WONDER? THE BLOKE CAN'T TALK ANYTHIN' BUT SENSE!

CHOP

REASONIN' WITH 'IM IS A GREAT IDEA, IF ONLY YOU COULD GET TO 'IS REASON WITHOUT LOSIN' YOUR OWN!

Smythe

DON'T YOU FIND IT SLIGHTLY BORIN', JUST LAZIN' ABOUT THE HOUSE ALL DAY?

2-5

IT DOES GET ON ME NERVES A BIT, PET — BUT EVERYBODY 'AS THEIR TROUBLES, DON'T THEY?

THE HORRIBLE THING IS, 'E'S *SERIOUS,* Y'KNOW

Smythe

3-15